Philosophies of Iconic Leaders

100 Foundational Truths To Center Uplift and Inspire Conscious Leaders

By Christy Rutherford

Philosophies of Iconic Leaders

ISBN-13: 978-1540528612
ISBN-10: 1540528618

First Edition for Print November 2016

Dedication

God, for the work you've done in me to embrace my uniqueness

My family, for showing me leadership early in life as leaders at work and in the community

Mastermind Members, Kenyon, Calvin and Jason, thank you for believing in me when I didn't believe in myself

Table of Contents

Foreword

When I met Christy nearly two years ago, we instantly connected. We shared a common trait - an uncommon and insatiable appetite for high levels of achievement and success. It's rare to meet other women who have an intense drive for high achievement, so meeting Christy was refreshing. I have often been questioned and made to feel guilty about my intense drive for a considerable part of my life. Christy allowed me to relax about some of the guilt and judgment because I learned then that I was not alone.

We have both invested a considerable amount of time, energy and money into enhancing our personal and spiritual development. In doing so, we have raised our levels of consciousness, vibrations and can offer our gifts and talents to the world in greater ways.

As we've become good friends, I'm continually fascinated by her background, experiences, shortfalls and the evolution into who she is today. Christy is a leader of leaders and has a unique perspective to offer, not only from what she achieved in her previous career but the thousands of hours she's invested in studying the principles and philosophies of great leaders.

As a Law of Attraction enthusiast, I've taught thousands of people about the power of vision and living their dreams. At a certain point in our lives, we stop dreaming. We stop reaching for the stars, because of the fear of failure and the unwillingness to work hard to make the dreams come to fruition. My mentor Dr. Myles Munroe once said, "Your future is not ahead of you, it's within you. We keep looking for our destiny, when in fact, our destiny is screaming at us saying, 'Let me out!'"

Christy is living out the vision in her heart, which is to inspire the next generation of leaders and assist leaders who are overwhelmed. You have a dream in your heart too and I urge you to give yourself permission to dream. Write the vision and make it plain. Start associating with people that will force you to believe in your dream and will encourage you to do the impossible.

Christy is a trusted confidant and I hold her counsel in high regard, because she lives what she teaches and together, we serve leaders all over the world. I'm honored to be a part of her newest work.

Keshelle Davis
The Training Authority
Master Trainer
Creator of "Standout & Make it Real" and "Dreamboard Parties"

Preface

In an ever evolving and rapidly changing world, great leaders are needed more than ever. At work, leaders are responsible for their individual roles, working as collaborative team members, providing timely and relevant feedback to employees, maintaining a highly engaged workforce and ensuring world-class customer service. At home, leaders are responsible for leading their household and ensuring their family's needs are provided for. In the community and in their industry, leaders create a ladder behind them, by providing mentorship and inspiration for future generations.

Leaders need to have confidence and grit, yet exude the qualities of a great leader to be truly effective. Leaders also need to be uplifted and provided with positive and relevant information to maintain overall balance. Not well balanced, a leader can work to their personal detriment.

Over the past four years, I've read countless books, listened to and watched thousands of hours of audios and videos from some of the world's greatest leaders. The time invested has led me back to my authentic self and allows me to stand in who I AM today unapologetically.

In my studies, I've noted there is a common thread that runs through highly successful leaders, regardless of ethnicity, gender, religion, country of origin, etc. There is a well-defined roadmap to success and high achievement. I also realized that most highly successful leaders were unpopular as they ascended the ladder. Many leaders are misunderstood and harshly judged until their visions are realized and impact others in great ways. Even then, a large number continue to be highly criticized.

Many self-made millionaires and billionaires rose out of impoverished conditions, had traumatic experiences, immense setbacks, and failures, but still managed to break the chains of mediocrity and achieved the success they desired. Money doesn't determine success, but at times, the measurement of money is based on the number of people that benefit from the gifts the leaders bring to the world.

Success is not handed to anyone on a silver platter. It must be fought for, bled for, cried for, sacrificed for and earned through persistence over an extended period of time. The biggest difference between highly successful leaders and those who fail is the people who gained success never quit; even in the face of pain, backstabbers, haters, critics and sabotage from family and friends. It's a tough road, but it's POSSIBLE.

Leaders Are Overwhelmed

Deloitte's 2014 Global Human Capital Trends report stated, "Sixty-five percent of executives...rated the 'overwhelmed' employee an 'urgent' or 'important' trend, while 44 percent said that they are 'not ready' to deal with it." The report also stated, "Senior executives should create a culture that broadens the opportunity for leaders to develop in new ways...continuously coaching and supporting leaders so they can build their capabilities as rapidly as possible."

On one hand, senior executives need to continuously coach and support leaders, and on the other hand, employees are overwhelmed and executives are not ready to deal with it. This highlights a gap, which I consider the proverbial elephant in the room, the human side of leadership. Senior executives may be overwhelmed too! Leaders carry high levels of stress and anxiety but have to show up to work every day and be the leader that everyone else needs while neglecting their own.

When people talk about how leaders should perform and act, they are stating what the perfect model of leadership should look like. This is great in theory, but when you add the human element, you don't account for the other roles leaders have to play in their lives. To "coach and support" leaders, takes an investment of time and/or money on the part of the leaders and organization.

Known as a leader of leaders, I invested a significant amount of time into my personnel and 70+ people outside my office.

Every evening, I spent 1-3 hours (at their request) sharing insight, leadership principles, balancing work and home, managing stress and anxiety, averting depression, and filling them with enough information that would last 15+ years. At home, late in the evening and on the weekends, I coached the other 70.

To complete all my tasks, lead and nurture, create and maintain a climate of fairness and respect, my personnel were adequately coached. However, I was overwhelmed, stressed out and had high levels of anxiety. I hid it behind a masked smile at work. No one checks on their heroes' well-being.

If you had an opportunity to read my previous book, *Shackled To Success*, you would see that I worked exhaustively to my personal detriment. For a number of reasons, I burned out. However, what accelerated the burnout was not being able to handle critics, bad bosses, and not growing and developing personally. Had I known that all great leaders have identical challenges, I would have realized I was amongst great company and not feel so isolated.

How many leaders carry the guilt and burden of missing important milestones in their family's lives because they were at work? How many have failed or strained relationships and marriages because they take work home and are not emotionally present? How many have unresolved guilt for missing time with their aging parents, only to show up to put them in a nursing home or attend their funeral?

Time can never be recouped and carrying this baggage, along with meeting the demands at work, not being fully engaged at home, all while coaching others, can be a significant contributing factor to the overwhelm leaders experience. Companies spend billions of dollars annually developing leaders professionally, but is anyone addressing the personal baggage leaders carry?

Leaders Set The Example
Regardless of the countless number of assessments and training programs available, people look for others with leadership traits they want to emulate. A great leader can cross

cultural, racial, gender and generational barriers. People are inspired by leaders with the traits they desire and look forward to growing into a similar mold.

If organizations don't have leaders that others want to emulate, there are going to be issues. If senior executives don't have the time or desire to deal with overwhelmed leaders (or themselves), is it realistic to expect a succession of leaders created in their organization? Is it surprising that the culture is dysfunctional, with leaders who can't seem to get along and employees that aren't fully engaged? Creating a pipeline of effective leaders starts with addressing the overwhelm, stress and anxiety that leaders face daily, but will not admit to.

"Awareness is the greatest agent for change."
- Eckhart Tolle

How Leaders Are Built

If you're a leader, are you willing to admit that you're overwhelmed? Only when you're willing to submit your ego and admit it, will you be able to change. A large part of it may not be your fault, but if you accept responsibility for where you are now, you can expect to see different results if you're willing to do some work.

I have a question for you. How did you develop your leadership style? What were the main building blocks that got you to where you are today? If you're like most leaders, your leadership style reflects this image. Using a building as an analogy for our career - in the beginning, we fly by the seat of our pants and use scrap material or anything someone is willing to give (advice, time, money) to build our career. Our wires (knowledge, heart, self-esteem, confidence, etc.) are exposed and all over the ground.

For the next few levels, we model the blueprint of success from others (what we see in leaders we admire, our office, homes, magazines, tv). As we progress and get more experience under our belts, we become more solid in our careers and build it with brick.

Reaching the higher levels, we finally build a penthouse and have windows and a balcony. It all looks great from the top, but the problem is with our foundation and early stages. The unstable and mismatch structure is reflective of our inner being and self-image. Even if we are in a penthouse, we can be a mess internally, regardless of what we've achieved externally and materially.

Also, since our wires are exposed, we are subjected to manipulation by people cutting our power, plugging themselves in or stealing the cables.

Can you relate? Does your leadership persona look like this?

Who Is This Book For?

My goal with this book is to share the principles and philosophies of Iconic Leaders, to give you insight on what they learned about themselves and others along their journey of success. To learn from them and use their hindsight to illuminate the road to success in front of you.

You'll also get a glimpse into their early lives and successes with a brief bio, but I encourage you to study them more in depth if you enjoy what they say and it resonates with you. These leaders have countless lessons to offer, but I highlight 10 quotes, followed by how I interpret what they said based on my background and experiences. Since we are all unique and have different perspectives, you may interpret their quote in a different way, and that's perfectly okay.

This book is intended to grow, develop and nurture you in ways that you need in order to survive being a great leader. Leadership is tough, but it's so AMAZING! May this book provide you with insight that will alleviate the burdens and baggage you carry and allow you to show up as a greater version of yourself to inspire the next generation of leaders.

The leaders featured in this book have added to my life immensely and I hope that it will add to yours. If any of these quotes speak to your soul, I recommend you write them out on 3x5 notecards and hang them in your bathroom mirror, around your house and at your office. Keep them as a constant reminder of what you need to do to take care of yourself and your mindset.

Each featured leader has books, videos, and audiobooks, so I encourage you to give yourself the gift of personal development and invest time into learning from some of the world's greatest leaders. I'm excited about what you will discover about yourself and how you will use it to expand what's possible for you.

You are a **L-E-A-D-E-R**. Let's unite and use our gifts to illuminate the light in others all around the world. It's time!

Chapter 1

Napoleon Hill

I often wonder how different my life would be today if I would have discovered Napoleon Hill in college. As someone who is obsessed with success and leadership, Napoleon Hill offers tremendous insight into what it takes to be successful and how to become wealthy. Many millionaires attribute their success and wealth to Napoleon Hill. His books, audiobooks, and videos offer the roadmap to success and if followed precisely, you can achieve anything you can imagine. You are only limited by how you view yourself and your circumstances.

If you haven't had an opportunity to read any of Napoleon Hill's books, I highly recommend *Think and Grow Rich*, *17 Principles of Success* and one of my personal favorite books OF ALL TIME, *Outwitting The Devil*. Read his books and apply the information, and I guarantee your life will never be the same.

*Oliver Napoleon Hill was born in 1883 and grew up in poverty in Wise, VA. Hill's mother passed away when he was 10 years old. His father eventually re-married an educated woman, who instilled in him that he had the ability to accomplish more in life.

When he was 15, he became a freelance reporter for a group of rural newspapers and later a popular periodical that offered advice on achieving power and wealth. An interview with 73-year-old Andrew Carnegie, the richest man in America at the time, changed his life.

Wealthy Carnegie asked an impoverished Hill to interview and associate with 500 of the most successful and wealthy people of that era. Carnegie suggested that there were certain behaviors and characteristics that wealthy people exhibited, that the poor and middle class didn't. He wanted Hill to work over a 20-year period, without pay, to develop a wealth philosophy that could be shared with the world and give everyone an opportunity to achieve wealth.

Carnegie introduced Hill to Henry Ford, the Wright Brothers, William Wrigley Jr., Charles M. Schwab, Theodore Roosevelt, John D. Rockefeller, J.P. Morgan, Thomas Edison and many more. By associating (hanging out) with them at their jobs, in their homes, with their families and other places, Hill was able to extrapolate their characteristics, traits, and actions.

After years of massive failures, heart break and triumphs (including an assassination attempt), Napoleon Hill successfully published a number of books, magazines, and articles. Think and Grow Rich was published in 1937 and by the time the Depression was over, more than 1 million copies were sold. Think and Grow Rich is Hill's greatest work and is considered the best self-improvement book of all time, with more than 30 million copies sold worldwide.

His philosophy for personal achievement can be summed up as, "If you can conceive it and believe it, you can achieve it." He personally earned millions of dollars by acting on and implementing the philosophies of success he gathered. (source Success.com)

His legacy continues with the Napoleon Hill Foundation, which provides scholarships to students at the UVa-Wise and other philanthropic efforts around the world. Go to www.naphill.org and sign up for their daily emails, newsletters and learn more about Napoleon Hill and his legacy that continues to impact millions of people long after his death in 1970.
******

Before trying to master others, be sure you are the master of yourself.

As a leader, are you willing to complete the tasks that you assign to others? Do you want people to respect you for your leadership position, regardless of your personal action and character as their leader? There is nothing worse than having an immature or untrained leader in a position of authority. This person can wreak havoc on an organization, create a toxic work

2

environment, an atmosphere of anxiety and stress, and cause personnel to look for other opportunities. It's well known that people don't leave bad jobs, they leave bad leaders.

If you're a leader and are having challenges with others following you, are you willing to look in the mirror to see if the issue is you? If you are daring, talk to a well-respected person who has been with the organization the longest. They've seen different leadership styles and know what motivates the workforce in that company culture. Ask them how they view you as a leader and the suggestions they have for you to improve your effectiveness with the workforce.

Work on yourself to expand your leadership knowledge. Change your approach in the way that you lead people and you'll find that people will change their minds about you and follow you anywhere when you BECOME a leader worth following.

Who told you it couldn't be done, and what great achievements has he performed that qualified him to set up limitations for you?

When seeking to get to the next level or achieving a new goal, you should be careful about who you get your advice from. Are you allowing family and friends to plant seeds of fear and failure in you? Do you have negative colleagues that give you all the reasons you can't achieve your goal? When you buy someone's opinion, you buy their lifestyle. If you were looking to buy a Mercedes S550, would you seek advice from someone who drives a Dodge Neon? Same applies for your goals. Seek advice and counsel from someone who has achieved the results that you desire.

Your mind is the only thing you can control exclusively. Don't give it away too freely to useless arguments.

There are people in organizations that make it their personal mission to fight every battle, regardless of whether or not the outcome affects them directly. Giving energy to useless arguments and situations, or circumstances that are not in your control is unwise. It also creates preventable stress and anxiety that you are subjecting yourself to. If your input to an undesired situation has the ability to change the outcome, then that's a battle worth taking up and backing with factual data. However, the information should be presented in a professional manner in order to be received properly. If talking about it or complaining won't change the outcome, then consider putting that energy and time somewhere that will yield the results to keep you ascending in the organization.

Before opportunity crowns you with success, it usually tests your mettle through adversity.

Thomas Edison failed at inventing the lightbulb 10,000 times. Walt Disney filed bankruptcy several times and was told he lacked imagination. A television station asked Oprah to change her name, stating that she would be received better. It's rare that someone has ever achieved massive success without failing greatly and mightily on numerous occasions before finally breaking through to success. Knowing this, there are two choices to make, play it safe and never attempt anything outside of your comfort zone, or go after your goals with everything you have, expecting to get knocked down…several times. Continue and go all the way through the goal until it is achieved. Napoleon Hill also said, "A man is never whipped until he quits in his own mind."

The individual who has time only for gossip and slander is too busy for success.

Successful people are always looking for the next mountain to conquer and rarely have time to nit-pick and talk about others. They are too busy looking ahead and not looking behind or around them to find fault and talk about others. Successful people also realize that giving negative energy to any situation, creates negative energy and circumstances in their lives, so they mainly focus on the positive. If you desire to get to the next level, and can't figure out why you are meeting resistance and/or have obstacles, evaluate how you treat other people.

If you have no major purpose, you are drifting toward certain failure.

Your job may not be your major purpose. It's a means to pay your bills, but it's not why you are here in this lifetime. Many people get caught up in the cycle of the 9-5 and lose sight of becoming who they dreamed of. Although you may be deemed "successful" when it comes to position, money and material possessions, you have not achieved the true success that comes with working in your purpose. Working in purpose, you are doing what you fills you with passion and wakes you up every morning ready to conquer the world.

It's never too late to work on your major purpose. Vera Wang started designing clothes at 40 and Colonel Sanders franchised KFC at 62. What would give your life meaning? Can you volunteer your time to a cause you feel strongly about?

You don't have leave your job to do what gives you meaning. Consider spending less time watching television and more time investing in what brings you joy. Each day, aspire to live your life full and without regrets.

It takes more than a loud voice to gain respect for authority.

There are some leaders who yell at their personnel in order to move them. It's not only disrespectful to them, it eventually erodes their motivation and self-esteem. It's also tiring for the leader. If you find that the only way to get people to do what you want them to do is by yelling at them, consider discovering what else motivates them. Is it public praise by acknowledging their good work versus always pointing out the bad? Are you giving them room to grow and the ability to learn from their mistakes, versus minimizing them and treating them as derelicts; and then get frustrated because they continue to be derelicts?

You can never go wrong by shifting the way that you talk to people and treating them like who you want them to become.

Treat people like they are two positions above their current position and provide mentorship opportunities for them to grow. You may be surprised that the majority of them will grow into the role you set for them and their behaviors will change too.

Get the audiobook, How to Win Friends and Influence People, by Dale Carnegie and listen during your commute. Take note of the insight he offers and use it regularly. You'll see noted change in others and yourself.

It is always better to imitate a successful man than to envy him.

There are a number of people that dislike highly successful and wealthy people. This is unfortunate because you have drawn a line in the sand and classified it as "us" and "them." Read Forbes 400 and you'll find that most self-made billionaires were born in poverty and overcame insurmountable obstacles. They are now enjoying the fruits of their labor. Success principles are universal and apply in any vocation. Study successful people and you'll find that most of them applied similar principles to achieve their dreams. Apply them to your life and watch it unfold in new and exciting ways.

Wise persons are those who think twice before speaking once.

This is not only a cliché, it's a skill that needs to be exercised on a regular basis. People lose positions and credibility when speaking out of turn. Also, some people think that by over talking others and solely talking about themselves and their accomplishments is impressive. It has the opposite effect.

In Master Networking by Tracey Smolinski (the UK's Queen of Networking), she shares great insight about the do's and don'ts when it comes to networking. Tracey suggests that you find the balance between listening and talking. She said, "People like to talk about themselves, so let them, it's not just about you!" Opportunities are created by your ability to make a genuine connection with others, and that starts with listening.

Don't covet the other fellow's job if you are not prepared to accept the responsibility that goes with it.

Do you look at your boss and think you would do better? Do you resent your coworkers, because they make more money than you, but do less work? Instead of harboring negative feelings towards others, find out how they got the position and what credentials they hold, and start at once in obtaining them.

Are you willing to do the work to get to their positions, or have you become content with just complaining about something that you can change? If you increase your qualifications and certifications, they will open up new possibilities for you; even if it's with a different company. The key is growing into the person that would fit into the position you desire, even if you have to switch jobs. Both require ACTION.

When men first come into contact with crime, they abhor it. If they remain in contact with crime for a time, they become accustomed to it, and endure it. If they remain in contact with it long enough, they finally embrace it and become influenced by it.

Have you become negatively influenced by your work environment? If you are in a toxic work environment, you could be toxic too and unconsciously take that negativity home. It can affect every area of your life.

Using a fish tank as an analogy, with a filter and regular cleaning, the water remains clear and the fish are healthy. If you start to inject black ink (negativity) into the water (office environment), the change won't be immediately apparent. But as the ink continues to be injected day after day, it will go from being a gray tint to dark and murky. Since the ink is now within the environment, it will start to penetrate the skin and organs of the fish, causing toxic reactions (stress, anxiety, depression, misery, anger). If the fish are still alive in the murky and dark water, they won't thrive and will eventually go belly up.

If you feel like your work environment (or home) is negative, you need to take a serious look at yourself and determine if you've been influenced by it. You could always ask someone at work who doesn't really like you, they won't spare your feelings.

O Divine Providence, I ask not for more riches but more wisdom with which to make wiser use of the riches you gave me at birth, consisting in the power to control and direct my own mind to whatever ends I might desire.

If you pray at night or during the day, are you asking for more money? Are you overwhelmed and think that more money will alleviate your problems?

If you aren't happy now, more money won't make you happy. Choose instead to pray about using your thoughts and mind to dig yourself out of the self-made prison hole you may find yourself in. Money isn't the answer to your prayers. Taking control of how you view the world and how others treat you is.

Chapter 2

Oprah Winfrey

Oprah is loved and admired by millions of people around the world. I watched her show periodically in the late 80's and 90's, but when I started watching her in 2008, my life took a dramatic shift. I was open and prepared to receive the spiritual teachers she hosted like Louise Hay, Eckhart Tolle, Gary Zukav, and Elizabeth Gilbert. Watching her show, reading her magazines and book club picks, changed the trajectory of my life. It wasn't an immediate shift, but a gradual learning and growth experience.

Unknowingly activating the Law of Attraction led to a culmination of events which caused me to resign from my career. Looking back, the "perceived challenges," moved obstacles out of the way and cleared the way for me to step into my destiny. Oprah has had an immense impact on my life and I hope that you've had the opportunity to be impacted as well. Check out her television network OWN, O' Magazine, her book and website.

*Television host, producer, actress, philanthropist and entrepreneur, Oprah Winfrey was born in Mississippi in 1954. She grew up in a small farming community and eventually moved to live with her father after being sexually abused by several male relatives and friends of her mother. She became pregnant, but suffered a miscarriage and carried the shame of being a pregnant teenager for years.

In 1971, she went to Tennessee State University and began working in radio and television broadcasting. She later hosted a show in Baltimore and was recruited by a Chicago television station to host her own morning show. After reading the book, *The Color Purple*, she became obsessed with it, saying it was a story that reflected her childhood. Through the Law of Attraction, she manifested a role in the 1985 movie, for which she was nominated for an Academy Award for Best Supporting Actress.

The following year, she launched the *Oprah Winfrey Show* and with an audience of 10 million people. The show grossed $125 million by the end of its first year, and Oprah received $30 million. She soon gained ownership of the program from ABC, drawing it under the control of her new production company, Harpo Productions (Oprah spelled backward) and ran the show for 25 years. She ended the show in 2011 and started her own network, the Oprah Winfrey Network (OWN). After a rocky start, the network has grown in notoriety and success.

According to Forbes magazine, Oprah was the richest African American of the 20th century and the world's only African American billionaire for three years running. She was named the "Most Influential Woman of Her Generation," by *Life* magazine and the "Greatest Black Philanthropist in American History," by *Business Week* in 2005. Her Angel Network has raised more than $51,000,000 for charitable programs, including girls' education in South Africa and relief to the victims of Hurricane Katrina.

In November 2013, President Barack Obama awarded Oprah the nation's highest civilian honor, the Presidential Medal of Freedom. (source Biography.com)
******

The way through the challenge is to get still and ask yourself, 'What is the next right move?'…and the next right move, and not to be overwhelmed by it, because you know your life is bigger than that one moment.

When you are in the midst of a storm or feel like you have fallen in a hole so deep you'll never get out of, it's hard to see the light. Trust me, I've been there. It can feel like you are drowning on dry land and no one really knows. At that moment, you feel toppled by your challenges, but Oprah offers great advice here. She asks, "What is the next right move?"

What do you need to do to solve your issue? Who do you need to get rid of and what do you need to let go of? What is the next right MOVE? When you figure out what you need to do, you need to take ACTION. It doesn't have to be massive action, but one step. If you're paralyzed by fear, taking one step will be tough, but do it. Once you take that step, you'll then be able to assess from a different view. Then, make the next right move and the next right move.

Eventually, you'll be able to see your situation clearly, but the key is moving. If you feel stuck, take a step. Do something, ANYTHING! Every challenge that you have can be solved with action, but you have to do it for yourself. No one can save you, but you.

There is a supreme moment of destiny, calling on your life. Your job is to feel that, to hear that, to know that.

When the moment of destiny comes, it usually comes at a devastating and painful time. Pain moves people into action, but if you misinterpret the call, you may feel like a victim. A layoff may look like a crisis, but if you've been wanting to start your own business, and didn't have the courage to quit your job, you got what you wanted.

A spouse leaving may be devastating, but if you've been unhappy for 5-10 years and felt unloved and unloveable, this moment may open the door to the love of your life.

When my moment of destiny came, it came with me resigning from a career that I loved, with only a few years left to retire. It was a devastating time, but looking back, it was all necessary in order to thrust me into destiny. The moment will not be convenient or comfortable. Comfort never moved anyone into action; only a breaking can do that.

There is no such thing as failure, really, because failure is just that thing trying to move you in another direction. So you get just as much from your losses as you do from your victories because the losses are there to wake you up.

If you failed at getting a job or achieving a goal that you set for yourself, what did you learn? There is a lesson in every single failure that you'll encounter in life. However, most people replay the failure over and over again in their mind, instead of finding the lesson in it. Once you find the lesson, use it to move to the next level, otherwise, you'll become stuck and stagnant.

Also, failing means that you are working and doing something. People who play it safe and don't do anything different don't fail. Be the exception.

Be aware of the energy you are putting out in the world.

Do you bring light, joy, and happiness into your workplace and home, or are you the darkness? Do you have a natural scowl on your face and complain all the time? Are you a part of the social media mafia and criticize others for what they do?

Darkness cannot drive out darkness, only light can do that. If you want more happiness and freedom in your life, then that's what you must give. By creating joy in the lives of others, it creates joy within you. If your life isn't going the way you desire and you feel like there's a negative cloud following you around, check yourself and see what environment you're creating for others. The life you desire starts and ends with you.

You don't have to hold yourself hostage to who you used to be or anything you ever used to do; cause who has lived and hasn't made mistakes?

A broken past doesn't have to keep you from living the life you desire. Do you feel like what happened to you in your childhood affects you today? Does it really or is it just the "story" about your childhood stopping you?

Everyone's had a crummy life, in some way or another, but some people choose to change the way they see themselves. They lift themselves out of that sad story and move into victory. Will you do the same?

Real integrity is doing the right thing, knowing that nobody's going to know whether you did it or not.

How many people do you see on social media who do a random act of kindness, that's not so random since they broadcast it to the world? Doing the right thing can be as simple as taking your shopping cart back to the store and not leaving it wandering in the parking lot to ding someone else's car.

Are your actions causing others joy or inconvenience? If a cashier gave you too much money, would you return it or stick it in your pocket saying that's their bad? Do you throw gum on the ground, causing someone to step in it and track it in their car?

One thing that's definite, is EVERY action you take in life creates a reaction. When you do good for others, Karma will repay the same to you. When you cause others pain or inconvenience, Karma will repay the same to you. Although "no one" may have known what you did, the books are always being kept by a higher source.

Lots of people want to ride with you in the limo, but what you want is someone who will take the bus with you when the limo breaks down.

If you are successful, then you may have a large circle of friends and associates. You don't know whether these people are around you for you, what you can do for them or what doors you can open for them.

Start to become mindful of who you surround yourself with. Will they be there for you in the bad times, just as they are there for the good times. Unfortunately, sometimes you only find out who your real friends are when you run into hard times. Whether it's money, health or work, crisis shows you who your real friends are. It's not as many as you think. If you have flaky people around you and feel used by them, get rid of them at once! You will be better for it.

Do not allow yourself to be marginalized and defined by other people's agendas and intentions because the power of your story lies in your personal intention.

Do you allow other people to manipulate you into living the life they imagine for you? Do they influence your decisions and you somehow end up fulfilling their needs at your detriment?

Creating a "personal intention" is the key. What goals do you have for yourself? What do you want your life to look like in five years? Ten years? The clearer you become on who you are, why you're here and where you're going, the more you will come into alignment with your purpose. Living from a place of purpose allows you to set clear intentions on the impact you are meant to create in this lifetime. When you live from the clarity of that space, people can't manipulate your energy or make you feel small for not doing what they want you to do. It's AMAZING!

If you don't know what your passion is, realize that the one reason for your existence on earth is to find it.

TD Jakes said, "What bothers you the most, you were called to fix." What are you passionate about? What makes you say, "Someone needs to do something about this!" Is it mentoring youth, feeding the homeless, motivating leaders, creating art programs for schools?

Y-O-U are the someone that you've been waiting for! It's your passion, and what you were created to fix. That's why the solutions are easy and obvious to you and no one else.

It's Y-O-U! Knowing this, what will you do about it? Can you reinvest the time that you are giving to non-fruitful activities and work in your passion? The people you are meant to serve are waiting for you. Go NOW!

Be thankful for what you have, you'll end up having more. If you concentrate on what you don't have, you will never, ever have enough.

In a country (U.S.) where people spend most of their income and overextend their credit, there's something to be said about being grateful for what you have. Are you wishing and working for a six-bedroom house, and not giving thanks and gratitude for your three-bedroom house? It's likely a lot better than the one bedroom apartment you had post-college.

Most of us aren't grateful for what we have until it's taken away. Simple things, like health. People aren't grateful for the ability to walk until they develop a crippling condition. People complain about their job and coworkers until they're laid off.

What are you grateful for? Do you have your health, a roof over your head, a car, clean clothes and running water? With these things, you are better off than over 50 percent of the people in the world.

Start keeping a gratitude journal. Keep a small notebook or journal by your bed and before you go to bed at night, write down five things you're grateful for. When you become grateful for what you already have, you'll want less. You'll also open yourself up for greater things.

Chapter 3

Jim Rohn

Jim Rohn is an international treasure and like Napoleon Hill, I wish that I had known about him earlier in my career. There are so many common challenges that leaders experience, that when we learn from Jim Rohn, our lives would be greater. Not easier, but greater. He had a fantastic personality and delivers his lessons with charisma and wit. His books, audios, and videos on YouTube will provide you with timeless leadership lessons.

*Born to an Idaho farming family in 1930, Rohn's parents ingrained a work ethic in him that served him well throughout his life. He often shared the story of the day he turned his life around. He was 25 years old and a Girl Scout knocked on his door and asked if he wanted to buy some cookies. Since he didn't have $2, he lied and said that he already bought some. He expressed that he had gone to college, had a job and a family, but didn't have $2. He cried when she left and that painful experience changed the trajectory of his life. Later, he was introduced to network marketing and met a wealthy gentleman, Mr. Earl Shoaff, who became his mentor.

Over the next six years, he became a millionaire through network marketing. One day, Rohn was invited by a friend to speak and share his success story, which he titled "Idaho Farm Boy Makes It to Beverly Hills." It went over so well that he received more invitations and eventually became a paid speaker.

Jim Rohn is one of the founders and pioneers of the self-help and personal development industry. He impacted the lives of millions through his life-changing material and is widely regarded as one of the most influential thinkers of our time. He's authored countless books and created a wide variety of audio and video programs. He's motivated and shaped an entire generation of personal development trainers and hundreds of executives

from America's top corporations. He's inspired and mentored other personal development leaders such as Tony Robbins, Mark Victor Hansen and Jack Canfield. He died in 2009.
(source JimRohn.com)
******

Many people work harder on their job than they do on their future.

While seeking to get to the next level professionally, many high achievers sacrifice personal development for professional development. Developing yourself personally expands your awareness and understanding of self, so if something happens to your job, you won't feel like your future is ruined and will be more likely to move into another position with ease.

Spend five minutes complaining and you've wasted five.

It takes more energy to complain about a problem than it does to take action to solve it. One keeps you in a state of negativity and the other creates positive energy. Surprisingly, most people have solutions to the problems they complain about.

If it's your workplace, offer a solution to your boss and request permission to implement your recommendations. You'll make yourself stand out amongst your co-workers and develop a reputation as a problem solver. If it's in your personal life, get a book or a coach, or go to an event that will shift you out of the space you're in. Otherwise, you're just wasting time.

Some people lead such mediocre lives they don't know if they are winning or losing.

Even if you're deemed successful by way of position, your life can be considered mediocre if you aren't happy. People who proudly say they have "Golden Handcuffs" fit into this category. Houses, cars and other material possession have become more important than living a fulfilled life. They can't see that the house they thought would make them happy, has become an anchor and is the very thing that makes them go to a job they hate.

Are you wasting precious time? Tomorrow is not guaranteed for anyone and people in their 30's and 40's are checking out of here faster than the express checkout at a 4-star hotel. How will you use the time you have left to serve others and live the life you truly desire?

If you really want to do something, you'll find a way. If you don't, you'll find an excuse.

Leaders are relentless in finding solutions to challenges. This is what separates people who achieve high levels of success and those who remain stagnate. Find creative ways to solve common issues in your organization and you'll soon find yourself moving up.

If you're blaming others for why you can't get ahead in your organization or life, how long have you had that problem? How is that working for you? Look within yourself and discover the real reason you are not moving forward and take ACTION to change it. Don't complain about the same thing next year, that you've been complaining about for the past five.

You are the average of the five people you spend the most time with.

This is true for income, weight, education, etc. Are you surrounding yourself with people who limit your possibilities? The fear of criticism from loved ones and friends may keep you living small and not going after your dreams. The fear of doing something outside of your comfort zone can be magnified when you add the fear of criticism from people around you.

If you choose to do something different, don't share your dreams and visions with others. Go in the direction of your dreams and don't let anyone talk you out of it. Also, evaluate your inner circle and know that if you want to shift your life, you need to find a new circle.

Go to Meetup.com and meet some new people who won't remind you of your past every time you talk about your future.

The challenge of leadership is to be strong, but not rude; be kind, but not weak; be bold, but not bully; be thoughtful, but not lazy; be humble, but not timid; be proud, but not arrogant; have humor, but without folly.

People perform at the level they are expected to perform and if they are berated, called names or frowned upon, they will meet the low expectation. It also creates undue pressure, stress and anxiety. As a leader, if you treat them with high regard, (even those that perform at low levels), their performance will significantly improve and they will be happier and more productive.

If you want to get the best out of your personnel, make sure you treat them like you want to be treated. Nurture them and give them the best opportunity to be successful. To see a noted shift in your personnel, I recommend the following:

1. Have an open conversation
2. Set clear expectations of their performance
3. Get feedback on their short and long-term goals
4. Express appreciation of who they are
5. Tell them how they fit in the overall picture
6. Give them room to grow
7. Coach them on the goals they set for themselves

If you don't sow, you don't reap. You don't even have a chance.

With the Law of Sowing and Reaping, you reap what you sow. When you sow goodwill and fellowship into others, you expect for that goodwill to be returned. When you criticize and demean others on social media, that criticism will be returned. It may show up at work with your coworkers or boss. If you don't sow good seeds, why are you expecting a harvest?

If you want a mentor, but can't seem to find someone to assist you with getting to the next level, what have you done for others lately? If you don't feel like you have time to assist others, look at where you are spending your time currently. Be mindful of where you spend your time and learn how to say no if you won't receive a positive return on your time or efforts.

Some people have so given up on life, they've joined the Thank God It's Friday Club. How sad.
According to Gallup's 2014 State of the Global Workforce, nearly 87 percent of people worldwide go to jobs every day that they don't like. People deplore Mondays, celebrate Hump Day and drive like maniacs on Friday to get home or to their favorite watering hole. Only to start the cycle again a few days later.

What's stopping you from pursuing something you are passionate about? It's time to revisit the dreams you had for yourself when you were a kid and go after them. Reinvest your tv time into causes and organizations that bring you joy. We all have a limited time here, so each day is a gift to make a difference in the lives of others.

If you don't design your own life plan, chances are you'll fall into someone else's plan. And guess what they have planned for you? Not much.
Earl Nightengale said, "People with goals succeed because they know where they are going. It's as simple as that." Do you have a vision for what you want your life to look like five years from now - personally and professionally? If not, you're sitting on the passenger side of life and someone else is doing the driving. Not having a plan can leave you lost, stressed, or suffering from depression because you aren't happy about the results you're getting. Get into the driver's seat of your life and go into the direction you desire.

Everyday stand guard at the door of your mind.
Your life and the way you feel about yourself and others is largely based on your environment. We are what we eat, but we are also what we feed our brains. Guard your thoughts against dramatic and negative television and radio. If watching murder

mysteries make you paranoid that someone is going to murder you, how is that considered entertainment?

Consider turning off the tv and read books relevant to achieving your goals. Turn your car into a personal development university by listening to audiobooks during your commute. For every challenge you have (money, relationships, self-confidence, depression, anxiety), there is someone that's solved that problem and wrote a book about it.

Lastly, don't let others dump their garbage in your mind. If you spend hours on the phone trading stories with your friends, comparing whose day was worse, how is that helping you move forward? Reinvest that time into activities that bring you joy.

Some people don't do well because they major in the minor things.

The Pareto Principle (80/20 rule) has wide application - 20 percent of your efforts create 80 percent of your results. Also, 80 percent of your efforts create 20 percent of your results. Where are you spending the majority of your time and what are the results you're getting?

Get really clear on where you are investing your time, energy, efforts and resources and the return on those investments. From that list, determine which of those constitutes your 20 percent, and concentrate your efforts on what gets you the best return.

Chapter 4

Myles Munroe

I learned about Dr. Myles Munroe when he died in a private jet accident in November 2014. I started to see leaders that I held in high regard share their condolences, and say he was a long-time friend. When great leaders call someone a trusted friend and make heart felt comments about them, that person must be great too.

I researched him and started watching his videos on YouTube and quickly found out why he was loved by millions of people around the world. One of the things that resonated with me about Dr. Munroe is he talked about training leaders on the principles of leadership, and doesn't necessarily do it as a pastor. He does it from a leadership standpoint, because some people are turned off by religion. He finds a way to reach leaders and meet them where they are. I've shared his videos with numerous people in my network.

I've watched countless videos of Dr. Munroe and had the pleasure to befriend one of his disciples two years ago, Keshelle Davis, who wrote the Foreword to this book. I don't think it's a coincidence and I'm grateful for the value she's added to my life, as she shares with me what Dr. Munroe taught her. His legacy and lessons live on and will continue to do so for generations to come.

*Born in 1954 in the Bahamas, Dr. Munroe grew up in a two-bedroom house with eleven brothers and sisters. He said his parents had one bedroom and his sisters had the other, so he and his brothers had to find somewhere to sleep on the floor. He often talked about the poverty he grew up in, and that he knows what it's like to have roaches and rats as your best friends.

When he was 14 years old, their schools colonized and he and his classmates were harshly ridiculed by one of their teachers from Scotland. They were told they were half bred monkeys and that they couldn't learn sophisticated things. He was told he was stupid, he would never learn and that his brain wasn't developed right.

Dr. Munroe proved him wrong and graduated #1 from his high school, earned 3 Bachelor's degrees in 4 years, a Master's in 18 months and has been awarded 5 Honorary Doctorate degrees. He wrote 60 books, 48 of them became best sellers and he taught millions of people in 132 countries before his untimely death. The jet accident killed everyone on board including his beloved wife, Ruth. They have two children, who are continuing the legacies of their amazing mother and father. (source Dr. Munroe's videos/speeches)

******

Leadership is not based on how many people serve you, it's based on how many people you serve.

Leadership is not about position, it's about how many people you're serving and how many are better because they worked for you. When someone works for you, they should have the opportunity to reach their highest potential in your organization or outside of it.

So many times, managers stunt the growth of their employees to keep them loyal. Leaders aren't afraid of growing their personnel and grooming them because that's how you build a culture of loyalty. How are you treating your personnel?

True leaders don't create followers, they produce leaders. They help people find their gifts and their talents.

Many people are underutilized and unappreciated by their bosses. True leaders take the time to cultivate greatness in their personnel. Set aside time each week to invest in your personnel; whether it's one-on-one or in a group setting. Take the time to empower and motivate them, and they will prove that you were right about believing in them to achieve whatever you assign them.

Most leaders are not made in a day. They have to go through struggles, challenges, experiences, failure and getting back up. Leaders are products of time and frustrations. That's what makes a great person.

Leaders are not created in a day and are created through challenging times. What separates leaders from followers is that leaders get back up when they've been knocked down, regardless of how many times it happens. The greater the challenges and obstacles, the greater the leader will develop. This is such a critical part of the process.

Once you arrive at your leadership positon, remember that it took a lot of work for you to become who you are today, so as you watch the growth of your personnel, expect for them to fall down and make mistakes. Ensure that you're there to assist them with getting back on their feet quickly.

Most great leaders don't talk about their struggles while they are in it. They tell you when they are out of it. Followers talk about their struggles all the time.

Are you always talking about your challenges while you are going through them or do you wait until you've overcome them? You will rarely hear a leader complain about what they're going through while they're in the fire. You'll also rarely hear them talk about it when they're out of it, and when they do, it's typically used to teach. This is a clear distinction between leaders and followers.

Leaders disturb comfort. Leaders disturb traditions. They shake up the familiar and challenge the barriers people set. When leaders meet a barrier, they push and push until they break it and move it.

If you're a leader disturbing the comfort zone of others, expect resistance and naysayers. People don't like it when others come in and shake up the norm. If you understand this, then you'll know you're in good company when people dislike you.

Will you let uncomfortable people also make you uncomfortable and stop you from achieving your destiny?

Every person was born to solve a problem in their generation. Most people get a career and not a call, so our jobs become a prison, because we never find out what our work is.
This philosophy is true on so many levels. We were all created individually and unique for a reason. Our uniqueness, backgrounds and experiences shape what we're passionate about. What we are most passionate about is what we were called to do in this world. If you understood this, then you will understand that your uniqueness is on purpose and you were specifically designed for a reason to solve a problem in the world.

It's easy to say, "Someone should do something about (insert problem)." But, YOU are the person you are talking about and waiting on. Whatever you have the greatest problem with seeing happen again and again, you were called to fix it. Some callings are greater than others, but working a job is not a calling. It's a way to earn income, but many people get confused and think that they were meant to solely contribute to their jobs for 30-40 years.

When purpose is not known, abuse is inevitable.
When you don't know and understand your purpose, you will always feel like you are out of place and being taken advantage of. It's similar to using a brick of gold as a door stop or to stabilize an uneven table. The gold is very very valuable, but is being used in menial ways. The same applies to you. You may have taken a job outside of your passion to make a living. If you're dissatisfied, feel overlooked and like you're not fully appreciated in your job, are you the bar of gold being used as a door stop?

Abuse (abnormal use) is when you are living and working a job that you are no longer passionate about and feel dissatisfied. If you feel undervalued and bored, regardless of what you've achieved and the money obtained, it's time to start working towards your purpose.

One of the greatest tragedies in life is to watch potential die untapped.

Do you find yourself constantly saying, "One day I'm gonna..." How long have you been saying this and what dreams are you deferring? A better question is, what's stopping you from doing what you say you're going to do? Time? Money? Children?

We are given glimpses of what would make us truly happy and what we are supposed to do while we're here in this lifetime, but we often defer the tasks for many reasons. Some people say they want to write a book, but don't have time, yet, never miss an episode of their favorite shows. Some people say they will travel more when they retire, but then they retire and feel too old to do so. Some people say they will change careers when their children are in school, out of school, in high school, middle school or the multitude of ways people use their children as excuses for not living their dreams.

The problem with delaying your dreams is that you think tomorrow is guaranteed. You feel that a lifetime is guaranteed. There are people checking out of here every single day due to accidents and health issues. You don't know if tomorrow is guaranteed, and there is no magical door that will open and give you all the time, money and directions needed to fulfill your dreams.

Start today where you are and you'll find that your life will make room for you to accomplish your dreams.

Never allow someone to judge you based on their measurements or their test.

How many times has someone made you feel like you weren't good enough? Whether it was school, a job, a boss, co-worker, friend or lover, we've all been judged before and were told that we didn't measure up. Since we are all created unique and have distinct personalities, we all won't perform at the same level, regardless of the task.

When you allow someone to judge you based on their measurements, you are guaranteed to fall short on most occasions. World renowned motivational speaker Les Brown was labeled "educable mentally retarded" in elementary school and carried that label all through high school.

Most people judge you on a weakness where they have strength. But what about looking at your strengths, compared to their weaknesses? It will all even out at some point and let's face it, we are all dysfunctional in some way. We just have different dysfunctions that make us unique. Know and understand that you were made perfect, and your uniqueness is what will allow you to carry out the destiny that you were specifically designed for.

Great leaders make themselves unnecessary. The goal of leadership is to move on. The goal of leadership is to protect what you built. If it dies when you die, you are a failure.

In some instances, people in leadership positions ensure their job security by making sure they are irreplaceable. This is not the goal of a true leader. A true leader is loyal to the forward movement of the organization and ensures that if something happens to them, there will be someone ready to step in and take their place.

If you have this challenge, and can't let go, you will find that it affects you when you go home at night. If you're the only one that can do your job, you will always be called; even for minor issues. It also wreaks havoc on any plans you have for a vacation.

Succession planning and someone being able to step in during your absence is critical, because if something unexpected happens to you, and your team and/or organization is adversely affected and can't recover, you've failed as a leader.

Chapter 5

Eckhart Tolle

I read and listened to *A New Earth* after Oprah named it for her book club in 2008. This book is another life changer. What struck me about Eckhart Tolle's teachings was his insight about the ego and the voice in our heads. My ego at the time was running amuck and the voice in my head was a tyrant. Acknowledging these two things were happening and causing unhappiness, Eckhart Tolle gave me an opportunity to change.

Along with countless lessons in this book, another point was living in the present. Living in the now and not always wishing I was somewhere else. This information was further explored in his book, *Power of Now*. As a leader, these books created significant shifts in my life and leadership style.

*Eckhart Tolle is a German born (1948) spiritual teacher and author. He had an unhappy childhood since his parents fought regularly and eventually separated. Feeling alienated in a hostile school environment, he also experienced considerable fear and anxiety growing up in post-war Germany, where he played in bombed-out buildings.

Tolle eventually moved to England and taught German and Spanish. Troubled by depression, fear and anxiety, he started searching for answers for his life and studied philosophy, psychology and literature at the University of London.

At 29, after suffering from long periods of depression that he felt was almost unbearable, he had a life-changing epiphany. Recounting the experience, he said,

"I couldn't live with myself any longer. And in this a question arose without an answer: who is the 'I' that cannot live with the self? What is the self? I felt drawn into a void! I didn't know at the time that what really happened was the mind-made self, with its heaviness, its problems, that lives between the unsatisfying past and the fearful future, collapsed. It dissolved. The next morning I woke up and everything was so peaceful. The peace was there because there was no self. Just a sense of presence or 'beingness,' just observing and watching." (source Telegraph magazine)

He spent the next few years walking around in a deep bliss. He stopped studying for his doctorate and sat on park benches in Central London and just watched the world go by. Essentially homeless, he stayed with friends, in a park or at a Buddhist monastery. His family thought he was insane. As he sat on the benches, people started asking him questions, and over time he developed an active audience. He eventually transitioned into being a professional spiritual counselor and teacher.

Eckhart Tolle is a highly sought-after public speaker and teaches around the world. Many of his talks, intensives, and retreats are published on CD and DVD. Through EckhartTolleTV.com, he gives monthly talks, live meditations and answers questions from viewers. #1 *New York Times* bestsellers, *The Power of Now* (translated into 33 languages) and *A New Earth*, are widely regarded as two of the most influential spiritual books of our time. (source Eckhart Tolle.com)

******

If you have a strong ego, something good happens to an acquaintance of yours makes you feel bad. It's called envy. It's absurd, but that's how it works because the ego thinks "Something has been taken away from me because somebody else received something good." It's a complete illusion, but that's the madness of the ego.

Are you happy for your colleagues when they get a raise, a new house or a new car? Do you wonder how they can afford a new watch and why you can't? How does someone else getting something nice make you feel about yourself? Why?

Something good happening to someone else has nothing to do with you, but if you have a large ego, you will somehow find a way to make it about you. If this happens to you, I highly recommend reading *A New Earth*. It assisted me greatly with my ego. :-)

What a liberation to realize that the "voice in my head" is not who I am. Who am I then? The one who sees that.

Whether you will publicly admit it or not, we all have a voice in our head. Depending on your past, and what you're doing now, the voice can be a tyrant and talk you out of doing any and everything that will make you happy. It will say, "You're a loser." "You're going to fail." "Remember what happened last time."

That voice is a tyrant! Knowing that you are not the voice is LIBERATING because that means you can tame it. It's like having a tape recorder. You are the tape recorder, not the tape. You can replace the tape with a better story, but it takes effort and time.

Life isn't as serious as my mind makes it out to be.

Do you take yourself too seriously? Do you think that everyone is watching you and waiting for you to fail? Do you think that people have it out for you at work? Is this really true? How has this paranoia stopped you from living the life that you desire?

This is especially true if you have a high-level position at work or in your industry. You have to be mindful of what you're doing and who you're with, at all times, to ensure that you maintain the image and the facade of who you think you are. Living this way is mostly ego, but it also feels like you're in a cage at a zoo for the entertainment of others.

Life isn't that serious. Lighten up. Play in the rain and laugh until your stomach hurts. Life is too short to be miserable. One way to get out of a pit of despair is to play your favorite songs from childhood and dance.

Music has the ability to quickly shift your mood and make you happier. Madonna, Prince and Michael Jackson (from the 80's) are always good choices. Beyoncé and Lady Gaga are great choices too. The key is not to take yourself too seriously. Dance for 15-30 minutes until you feel better. If you have to dance until you pass out, that's a great option too!

You need to be alert and honest to find out, for example, whether your sense of self-worth is bound up with things you possess. Do certain things induce a subtle feeling of importance or superiority?

Well.....does it? Does your bigger house make you feel better than your colleagues? Does your luxury car with leather seats make you feel more successful than your employees that drive domestic cars with cotton seats?

There is a common misconception that who you are and your true value is based on what you have. That's simply not true. Your value and self-worth come from how you feel about yourself and the foundation is in character and integrity.

Do you treat people well? Do you relive a tragic childhood? Do you lie constantly?

If you have cracks in your character, no amount of money will fill them. Only by living a just and noble life will you find the true meaning of self-love.

You then unconsciously cling to the illness because it has become the most important part of who you perceive yourself to be.

Do you have a debilitating medical condition and blame it for everything that's going wrong in your life? Do you use it as a reason to feel sorry for yourself and stop trying?

"I am diabetic." "My lupus won't let me." "My arthritis has stopped me from..."

When you claim a condition with, "I am" and call it "my," you perceive yourself to be the illness and not yourself. You replace your name with the name of the illness and live from that space. Nothing great will ever come from that.

Choose to wrestle that illness to the ground and get your name back! Start saying that you are healthy, strong and healed. Believe it, meditate on it and you'll eventually find that your condition will adhere to what you say to it. Command it to go away and it will!

There are many people who are always waiting for the next thing to react against, to feel annoyed or disturbed about - and it never takes long before they find it... They are addicted to upset and anger as others are to a drug.
This is so timely for what's going on in society today. People are looking for reasons to be outraged and they can find a reason every single day. There is a group of people I call the "social media mafia," who troll social media to harass other people and destroy their careers and self-esteem.

In a world of cynics and critics, how are you showing up? Look for the joy and happiness in the world and you'll find it. Look for chaos and pain, you'll find that too. What are you looking for?

If you are awake enough, aware enough, to be able to observe how you interact with other people, you may detect subtle changes in your speech, attitude and behavior depending on the person you are interacting with... You are playing roles... In many cases, happiness is a role people play, and behind the smiling facade, there is a great deal of pain.
Do you live a life of authenticity? Do you know who you are and why you're here, all the way to the cellular level? If you did, you wouldn't change who you were to fit into different environments or when you talk to others. You would be able to treat the CEO the same as the janitor because you know that their positions don't define them. You would also know that you are no better than the janitor or worse than the CEO, because who they are have no impact on who you are.

When you compare yourself to others or when you don't know who you are at the cellular level, you aren't living authentically. You're also susceptible to wearing masks to fit it, switching them quickly to fit in with different groups of people.

Living like this is a life of misery and pain, even though you look good, smell good and smile. Do the work and get clarity on who you are and start making decisions from that place. Your life will significantly change for the best.

Give up defining yourself - to yourself or to others. You won't die. You will come to life.
Do you seek the advice and input of others before you make decisions and then take their advice, only to end up miserable? On another spectrum, do you debate with people when you make decisions about your life?

When you do this, you have made your life a democracy and are seeking the approval of others. This will keep you in bondage and misery, because the only person who knows what's really right for your life is you. Don't keep seeking the approval others at the expense of self-love and how you feel about yourself. Make decisions for yourself, even if it rubs people the wrong way.

As long as your decisions aren't directly inflicting pain on others, be okay with them being in indirect pain since you are no longer manipulated by them. Keep moving forward!

Unhappiness is an ego-created mental emotional disease that has reached epidemic proportions.
The number of people who are depressed, have panic attacks, and box wine drinkers have dramatically increased over the past 20 years. Teenage deaths from drug overdose is an epidemic. These numbers are becoming so significant that people are normalizing "mental illness" in college students, when it's really them experiencing life.

It's no coincidence the drama that people have in their life usually reflects their favorite reality show. Also, being in tuned to the latest celebrity gossip and fully engrossed in the lives of others.

Every minute that you spend looking at the life of others leaves you one less minute to look at your own. Turn off the tv and the negative radio. Reinvest that time into personal development and self-help books. You are the only person that can save yourself.

You will be free to let go of your unhappiness the moment you recognize it as unintelligent. Negativity is not intelligent.
It takes just as much energy to live happy as it does to be a pessimist, angry, jealous, resentful or mad. The challenge is shifting your mind from a dark space to one of light and freedom. This is a choice that you will have to make every single day when you get up. What will you choose?

Chapter 6
Michelle Obama

I can write an entire book about how First Lady Michelle Obama has set a new standard for how strong and intelligent women should carry themselves. She carries herself with such grace and is well loved by millions of people around the world. Even in one of the highest offices in the world, she's remained grounded, shares no-nonsense advice and encourages people to be great.

Michelle Obama is the most educated First Lady in the history of the U.S., and I love that she also happens to be a strong, beautiful and highly intelligent African American woman, raising two daughters. I have truly enjoyed watching the impact that she's had in the lives of others and I'm grateful for the impact she's had in mine.

*Michelle Obama is the 44th First Lady of the United States and wife of U.S. President Barack Obama. Michelle Obama was born Michelle LaVaughn Robinson in Chicago in 1964. Her father was a city-pump operator and her mother was a secretary at Spiegel's, but later stayed home to raise her and her older brother. They lived in a small bungalow on Chicago's South Side and the siblings slept in the living room with a sheet serving as a makeshift room divider.

Raised with an emphasis on education, Michelle Obama and her brother learned to read at home by the time they were four and both skipped the second grade. Following in her brother's footsteps, she attended Princeton University and later earned a degree from Harvard Law School. Following her graduation from Harvard, she worked at a Chicago law firm, where she met Barack Obama. They were married several years later and eventually had two daughters Malia and Sasha.

After working several high profile positions in law, she became the Associate Dean of Student Services at the University of Chicago and then the Executive Director of Community Relations and External Affairs at the University of Chicago Medical Center. She also served as a board member for the prestigious Chicago Council on Global Affairs, before transitioning to her role as the First Lady.

Quickly becoming a fashion icon that women around the world emulated, Michelle Obama was featured in *Essence* magazine as one of "25 of the World's Most Inspiring Women." In September 2007, she was #58 in "The Harvard 100," a yearly list of the school's most influential alumni. She's appeared on the cover of *Vogue* twice and made the best-dressed list for *Vanity Fair* and *People*.

As the First Lady, Michelle Obama has focused her attention on issues such as the support of military families, childhood obesity, healthy eating, exercise, poverty, and education. She's visited countless public schools, stressing the importance of education and volunteer work. As part of her mission to promote healthy eating, she released a book, *American Grown: The Story of the White House Kitchen Garden and Gardens Across America,* which explores her own experience creating a vegetable garden, as well as the work of community gardens elsewhere.

President Barack Obama, First Lady Michelle Obama, Sasha, and Malia have served as role models for millions of people around the world. The pure love they share and displayed for each other set a stellar example of family values. They will be missed as they transition out of the White House and into the next chapter of their journey in 2017. (source Biography.com)
******

If my future were determined just by my performance on a standardized test, I wouldn't be here. I guarantee you that.

Isn't this the truth! As you can see from her Ivy League education and high profile jobs, a standardized test doesn't adequately determine a person's ability to succeed. Frustrated with taking the SAT six times trying to score a 900, I thought that I wasn't qualified or smart. By the time I had taken the GRE a few years ago, I knew that I was intelligent, which was good to know because my score was laughable.

Intelligence and the ability to excel cannot and should not be determined by standardized tests. We all learn differently and these tests aren't an accurate measurement of you or your children's capabilities, so don't lose heart. Find a different way and go in the direction of your destiny.

I wake up every morning in a house that was built by slaves, and I watch my daughters, two beautiful, intelligent, black young women, playing with their dogs on the White House lawn.

This is a significant time in the lives of African Americans and I'm grateful to have witnessed this in my lifetime. I'm particularly grateful that my older family members who were subjected to hate, mistreatment and segregation in the 30's – 70's are still alive to witness the forward movement of African Americans in this country. Although we've moved forward, there is still A LOT of work to be done with regards to race relations in this country.

We learned about gratitude and humility - that so many people had a hand in our success, from the teachers who inspired us to the janitors who kept our school clean... We were taught to value everyone's contribution and treat everyone with respect.

It takes a village to raise a child and I'm glad that the First Lady recognized others in her success. You never know how the seeds you plant in others will manifest in their lives later on. Make sure they are seeds of greatness and inspiration.

I am an example of what is possible when girls from the very beginning of their lives are loved and nurtured by people

around them. I was surrounded by extraordinary women in my life who taught me about quiet strength and dignity.

Michelle Obama's mom sacrificed her career and became a stay at home mom. I'm sure the additional money would have been beneficial in the home, but there was a sacrifice made to provide her children with the tools they needed to be successful and loved.

There are plenty of parents that work in order to provide their families with big houses, fancy cars, and expensive clothes, but in the end, is it really worth it? *Presents* cannot replace *presence*. Presents cannot nurture self-love and self-esteem. How are you spending your time?

Women, in particular, need to keep an eye on their physical and mental health because if we're scurrying to and from appointments and errands, we don't have a lot of time to take care of ourselves. We need to do a better job of putting ourselves higher on our own "to do" list.

At home and work, women generally put everyone's needs above our own. We will make sure that everyone around us is happy, while we secretly die on the inside. We also don't do a good job at setting aside me-time. If you're overwhelmed, consider making yourself a priority.

If you're a man married to a woman who never complains, make sure you give her an opportunity to take care of herself. Give her monthly massages, flowers and ensure that she's taking care of herself. That way, she can better take care of you.

Barack and I were raised with so many of the same values, like you work hard for what you want in life. That your word is your bond. That you do what you say you're going to do. That you treat people with dignity and respect, even if you don't know them and even if you don't agree with them.

This is important because there's an alarming trend today where if people don't agree with someone, they attack them and their views. We all have unique experiences that shape our perspectives. Just because someone doesn't see the world or an issue the same as you, that doesn't make them wrong. It just makes them different. Can you respect a different point of view? If it's important enough, take the time to try and see the issue from their perspective?

Success isn't about how much money you make, it's about the difference you make in people's lives.

What is your definition of success? Has it changed as you've grown in your career? Are you using your success and what you've learned along the way to serve and inspire others?

Contributing to the lives of others will bring immense joy, but many leaders don't feel they have time. Make time in your schedule to mentor people at your office, in your community or at the local high school. We are responsible for shaping the next generation and we can't keep complaining about what they're not doing if we aren't willing to step in and show them the way.

How will you contribute to the lives of others during your lifetime? People won't talk about how many awards, cars or houses you had at your funeral. They typically talk about how you added value to the lives of others. What will people say about you?

You do not have to say anything to the haters, you don't have to acknowledge them at all. You just wake up every morning and be the best you can be, and that tends to shut them up.

Many people choose to give their energy and attention to people who don't like them. When people don't like you, it generally has nothing to do with you, but everything to do with how they feel about themselves. There is rarely anything you can do to gain the approval of someone who doesn't like you, so why bother?

Paying attention to them gives them power and it pleases them when they can inflict their pain on you. Instead of focusing on them, spend your time and energy focusing on how you can be a better person. Work to approve of and love yourself, and leave the haters where they are; in a ditch of misery and pain. Don't let them pull you in it.

Real men treat the janitor with the same respect as the CEO.
Do you change how you feel about people based on their position? Do you feel a sense of superiority when you're around others who aren't as successful or don't make as much money as you? Everyone has a role to play in this world and feeling differently about others doesn't reflect on their character and judgment, it reflects on yours.

In the previous chapter, Eckhart Tolle shares insight on the madness of the ego. Work to get clarity on your ego and improve the way you see yourself and it will significantly shift how you see others.

When they go low, we go high.
When someone says nasty things or criticizes you, what is your response? Do you engage in a negative exchange with them or express your negativity with others? Mark Twain said, "Never argue with stupid people, they will drag you to their level and then beat you with experience."

Grow and develop to the point that people can no longer bother you with their ignorance. It's a feeling of freedom like no other!

Chapter 7

Brendon Burchard

Two years ago, I got an email saying that Brendon Burchard was giving away his newest book, *The Motivation Manifesto*. The book was free, and I just had to pay shipping and handling. Never turning down a free book, I ordered it. Let me tell you something…this book is one of my top five favorite books of all time. I screamed out loud as I read it and ran out of ink while underlining important points. They're ALL important! I also carried it with me everywhere and would read it to others during extended car rides.

This book is raw and uncut and will give you a swift dropkick in the head if you need to be moved out of the space you're in. Brendon Burchard holds nothing back and goes all in on people that try to stop you from achieving your destiny. I suggest you add this book and his other books to your collection ASAP!!

*After suffering from depression and narrowly surviving a car accident at 19 years old, Brendon Burchard was bleeding, and stood on top of the crumpled hood of his wrecked car. He was faced with the concept of mortality and asked himself, "Did I live? Did I love? Did I matter?" He then decided to follow his dreams to become a writer and trainer. He failed for years and went bankrupt. However, he eventually persevered and became a multimillionaire by the age of 32. He's dedicated his life to helping others find their charge and share their voice with the world.

Brendon Burchard has been named "One of the Top 25 Most Influential Leaders in Personal Growth and Achievement," by *Success* Magazine. Oprah.com named him "One of the Most Successful Online Trainers in History." He's shared the stage with the Dalai Lama, Sir Richard Branson, Steve Forbes, Arianna Huffington and hundreds of other world leaders. He's authored

several *New York Times* bestsellers and is the executive producer of the #1 self-help series on YouTube. His seminars, "Expert Academy" and "High Performance Academy," sell out to audiences around the world. (source Brendon.com)
******

"They" start running our lives and soon we are not "us" anymore, just walking zombies filled with the commands of others' preferences and expectations. We become those masked souls who spend their time wandering in a wilderness of sameness and sadness.

Who are your "they" that stop you from living the life that you desire? Family and friends are included and have been known for holding millions of people hostage, leaving them playing small to fit it. It's been said that 90 percent of your friends won't attend your funeral. I saw this play out in real life when one of my friends died in a car accident.

I'm not sure if I can say this enough and reiterate it with quotes from other leaders, if you are playing small, adjusting who you are and not living in the fullness of your greatness, because of what "they" may say, it's time to find a new set of they! **They** should want to see you happy. **They** should want to see you expand into your destiny. **They** are not threatened by you wanting to grow into your full power. **They** will love you for who you are.

But what of the real tyrants and discriminators who hold us back, those who cause us pain when we try to move forward, those who prejudice against us because of our race, religion, gender, lifestyle, background? *To those bastards, we owe nothing.*

I love Brendon Burchard! How many people are you allowing to destroy your self-confidence and dreams, simply because they're tyrants? Misery loves company and people who are in pain love to inflict pain on others. Are you allowing them to make you a victim?

If your boss makes you miserable and is causing you physical pain, why are you still at your job? Can you get a different job in a non-toxic work environment or will you allow people to put you in your grave?

Research shows that if you work for a terrible boss (bully), and they have targeted you, there is at least an 80 percent chance that you will lose your job. Are you waiting around for the inevitable or will you take charge of your life and seek greener pastures?

But job titles, raises, "Mr." and "Mrs.," positions on advisory boards, and public acclaim rarely give us meaning... But what if we chase all that and believe in all that and then one day awake to find those things aren't what matter most.

Are you highly successful in your professional life? Do you have more degrees than a thermometer, but still feel like there's something missing? You may be missing the better part of yourself that you sacrificed for high levels of success. There are always trade-offs when it comes to achievement, yet many people don't talk about it.

By the results I produced, I was considered a fantastic leader, but was not a great aunt, because I missed my niece and nephews' birthdays for years. I knew my niece's birthday was May 10th, but didn't know when May 10th actually occurred. I was an okay daughter because I didn't visit home as often and every year, got progressively worse in picking out thoughtful Christmas gifts for my mom. Earlier in my career, we were in tune and I knew what she wanted. As time passed, I got busy. We talked less and I didn't know anymore. I was a pretty lousy niece and cousin because I was too stressed to manage my dramatic family during the holidays.

Are you operating on old data when it comes to your definition of success? Take some time and think about what success means to you today. Is it still about titles or is it about spending time with your aging family members. Only you can decide that for yourself. Once you define it, take ACTION to make it happen.

Locked indoors and hidden behind machines, we missed the entire season - the winter passed and we didn't play in the snow, the spring bloomed and we overlooked the flowers, the summer and the fall passed so quickly and we don't even remember the trees changing or feel satisfied with the time we spent outside.

The signal that summer has started usually comes when the kids are out of school and the buses aren't on the roads. Summer is over when they return. It's so easy to get stuck in a routine of driving to work in the dark and leaving when it's dark. Eating at your desk and then using the weekends to run countless errands.

I can honestly say that over the past few years, I've been astounded at the clouds, sky and stars. I wonder if mother nature had always put on a magnificent show every day or has it just been recently.

When is the last time you stopped to smell the roses? When was the last time you noticed the changing of the leaves in the fall or a rainbow after rain? When is the last time you've looked up to notice the multitude of cloud formations or stars?

What are the best parts of your life that you're missing out on? Take time at lunch, or in the afternoon to go for a walk. Tomorrow is not guaranteed for any of us, and to think otherwise would be naïve. Write down the goals you would like to achieve in this lifetime and start at once working on them. Work NEVER ENDS, but this lifetime will.

We mustn't be so numb or absentminded as to allow ourselves to suffer the fate and misery of those choosing a half-interested, half-engaged life.

So many times, we get stuck in routine and we are just going through the motions. Many people are BORED TO DEATH. People are infatuated with the series, "The Walking Dead," but the walking dead can be seen with some commuters on their way to work in DC, New York, and other cities. They are simply going through the motions without emotions or any feeling in their faces.

Are you stuck in a routine? Do you get up, go to work, go to lunch, go home, eat dinner, drink, and go to bed. Get up, go to work, go to lunch, go home, eat dinner, drink, and go to bed. How long have you been doing this and are you willing to break this pattern?

Make the decision to break away from the routine and do something different. Try something new on the menu at your favorite restaurant or choose a different place to eat. Switch up the times and routes you take to and from work. Do something, ANYTHING, to break the routine and monotony of life.

Eleanor Roosevelt said, "Do something every day that scares you." What two things can you do today to break your routine?

Everything we consume becomes a part of us. All the useless factoids and scandals do nothing but take root in our psyche and emerge as stupidity and drama later on.

If your mind is likened to a garden, what seeds are you planting? Do you want to have less drama in your life, but watch dramatic reality shows regularly? Do you want to worry less, but watch the news that highlights the world's atrocities on a 24-hour news cycle?

That's like wanting to grow peaches, but planting onion seeds. Knowing this, what will you do differently? Consider changing what you feed your mind with and you'll find that your life will change for the best.

Ultimately, those sad souls who believe that reality cannot be shaped do very little in life and will unfortunately be judged as weak, irresponsible, or forgettable.

Are you taking full responsibility for the results you have in your life? It's easy to look at outside circumstances and blame them for causing you problems, grief, anxiety or depression. Yet, the hardest thing to do is to look in the mirror and take 100% responsibility for what's good and bad in your life.

If someone has achieved the results you desire, then it's possible for you to do the same. Some people get mad at their coworkers, citing they should make more money than them because they are more talented and smarter. However, they haven't taken the time to evaluate HOW their coworkers got their salary and won't take the necessary steps to attain the credentials their coworkers have.

Take responsibility and take ACTION!! There are millions of books that give you the shortcut to success. Learn from the challenges and pitfalls of other successful people and shorten your learning curve.

Without more people deciding to serve as role models and leaders, our society has become a suffering case of the silent and bland leading the silent and bland.

It has become a societal norm to celebrate mediocrity and low level successes. Celebrating a child's First Grade Graduation and buying them gifts, taking their pictures and then taking them to dinner. I mean..... Really? Not saying that this wasn't good, but is that considered "achievement?"

With organized sports, everyone gets a trophy so their feelings won't be hurt because they lost. Growth generally happens with pain and if everyone gets trophies, then what it is the driving force behind becoming better? Losers are celebrated, if not more than winners. Also, winners are taught to not be too braggadocios, so it levels the playing field and dilutes achievement.

It's not too late to reverse this trend. If you're a leader, choose to become a mentor to others and inspire them to become leaders. Leaders aren't just born, they can be cultivated, but it takes an investment. I don't have children, so I won't offer advice on the trophies, but if I had kids, they wouldn't bring a trophy home if they lost.

Very few people have ever done deep work in defining their character - the specific identity they wish to have. They simply respond to the world on a whim, without paying any real attention to the type of person they want to be or become.

Who do you want to Be? Do you recognize yourself in the mirror? What would make you 100 percent proud to be you? In the pursuit of greatness and high levels of success, have you surrendered your character and your values?

It's not too late to Become who you desire, but it takes work. The first step is getting crystal clear on who you desire to be and how you want to show up in the world. Doing this is tough because you have to acknowledge some of the ugliness you may feel about yourself. You'll also have to finally admit that you can be better than you are today and that takes humility.

Take the hard road and take a good hard look at yourself and your heart. Get clear and do the work to make it happen.

It seems that a great tidal wave of cynicism and pessimism has washed ashore and drowned the dreams of our people. The emotional energy of the world is flatlining.

Social media and reality television have unleashed a wave of cynics, critics, and anger. It's like people are looking for ways to be offended, so they can unleash their pain and ugliness on others. Social media has allowed a collective voice of angry and bitter people to unite to seek and destroy anyone who does not believe in what they believe.

Every week, the media is reporting that people are "outraged." Whether it's the color of Starbuck's cups for the holidays, something an NFL player did or a prom dress a student wore, people are mad. The Washington Post released an article last year entitled, "Whatever Happened To The 15 People The Internet Hated Most In 2015?" TRAGIC!

When you participate in negativity, whether directly or indirectly, be aware that Karma is always keeping the books.

That negativity will be returned to you somehow, someday, some way.

Chapter 8

Holton Buggs

As I was shifting out of my previous career, I joined a network marketing company a few months earlier. Along with a host of other reasons, being around overworked and stressed out people daily drained my soul's batteries. When I was introduced to the people of Organo Gold, a company that distributes healthy coffee and teas, it's like a magical universe opened up. I eventually learned that people who were pursuing their dreams with relentless commitment and faith will light up any room.

Holton Buggs is the Executive Vice-President of Sales for Organo Gold International and was the first person that inspired me to become wealthy. He said that most people don't become wealthy because they don't think about it. I never thought about it. Becoming wealthy is not always about the money, but it's about who you BECOME along the way. Also, how you use the money to serve others. I traveled all over the country for two years to hear him speak and was inspired to change. Trading a good life to work towards a great life.

Mr. Buggs' goal is to touch and inspire 100 million people around the world directly and indirectly. I can honestly say that he's had a tremendous impact on my life, introducing me to the teachings of Napoleon Hill, Jim Rohn, Les Brown and countless others. He's also indirectly inspired you, as I share what I've learned. I am truly grateful for how he has positively impacted my family for generations to come.

*Holton Buggs grew up in the Ponce De Leon projects in Tampa, Florida. As a single parent, his mom worked multiple jobs to take care of him and his brothers. At 14 years old, he discovered the power of leverage by buying candy in bulk and recruiting people to sell it for him. One of the 12 people he recruited was Earlene Lilly, who's now Earlene Buggs, his wife, and best friend.

He attended college, majoring in Engineering and at 27 years old, he and Earlene started a furniture company. Although they had money, a nice house, and nice cars, he was time poor and felt like a slave to the business, because he felt like no one could do what he needed to be done better than him.

He was introduced to network marking, and worked hard for 7 years, never earning more than $500 a month. His organization never grew to more than 50 people and those 50 were not all in at the same time. He was eventually mentored from afar by a billionaire who earned a million dollars every 17 minutes in network marketing. After finding himself $250,000 in debt from their furniture business, 45 days away from foreclosure, and their Lexus was repossessed, he knew that something had to change.

He joined another company, and due to the right timing and having the foundational knowledge from years of "perceived failure," he and Earlene earned millions of dollars and assisted a few more families to do the same in a very short period of time.

After joining the team at Organo Gold and producing multiple six figures in sales, in less than a week, he was invited to join the leadership team. Holton Buggs is one of the top income earners in network marketing, and at one time, earned over $1.4 million a month. He was featured in *Millionaire Magazine's* Billionaire's edition in an article titled Millionaire Maker. He is a Master Trainer and speaker and has produced several audios, including the Cash Cow, which is a foundational audio for anyone in network marketing.

Mr. Buggs has extensive philanthropic efforts but doesn't advertise them. He's the Chairman of the Board of OG Cares, a non-profit that has impacted children in India, China, Nigeria, Mexico, New Orleans, Canada and other places around the world. He's also been known to buy all the fireworks at a fireworks stand and give them away to the children in underprivileged areas. At Christmas, he challenges people to "out give the giver," and will secretly pay for everyone's meal at a restaurant and tip the staff very handsomely.

Mr. Buggs is just an amazing person and whatever opportunity you have to see him speak in person, take it. He's also featured in videos on YouTube. He will inspire you to achieve greatness through the power of your thoughts.
(source HoltonBuggs.com)
******

If there is no target on your back, it means no one is aiming at you. If no one is aiming at you, it means no one is paying attention to you. If no one is paying attention to you, it means no one has interest in you. If no one has interest in you, it means you have got a lot of work to do!!! Embrace the Bullseye!

A lot of people are discouraged and hurt when people start talking about them. Naysayers, also known as haters, come out in flocks the more success and notoriety you achieve. Even if your goal is to solely serve and assist others, there will always be a group of people who won't like it. Can you handle success?

Knowing that all successful people have a group of haters should bring you relief instead of feeling isolated. People don't talk about mediocre performers, only winners. Embrace the Bullseye!!

A focused person with little talent can outperform a distracted expert every time in an extended race.

Talent and skills can be obtained with hard work and dedication. Education is not an indicator of success. It may open doors, but there are plenty of highly successful and wealthy people who did not graduate from college. It's all about focus and a commitment to success.

Are you committed to the long journey to achieve high levels of success? Commitment shows up in your actions and how long you're willing to work to get what you desire. If you are easily distracted and have the shiny object syndrome when you are looking for quick success, you won't be successful. Focus, dedication, and Becoming who you were meant to be while you're on the journey will guarantee success.

Too many people allow others disbelief to affect their own. Belief is not needed when you're up. Belief is needed when you have the desire to go up and are challenged.
Do you seek validation for your dreams from other people? Do you need the support of your family and friends before you step out and take a risk? No one will believe in you as much as you believe in yourself. If you're seeking support and validation from others before you make a move, you will be stuck forever.

When you have a vision stirring around in your heart, the only person that can make it come to reality is you. No one else has seen it or will understand the passion you have for it. Believe in yourself, believe in the impossible (I'm-possible) and go after the life you truly desire and deserve.

How many times do we blame everyone around us for our issues when the KEY to solving our issues is inside? Call someone with experience for counsel and they will help you find the answer inside of you.
When you have a problem, who do you get your advice from? Do you call your family and friends for advice or worse, seek advice from strangers on social media? When you buy someone else's opinion, you buy their lifestyle. When you get advice from someone else, you're likely only telling them one percent of the story. You're also usually seeking validation for the answer that you may have come up with on your own.

When you seek counsel, you are seeking insight from someone who has the results you desire. You're also working with someone (a coach) to unlock the hidden answer that is within you. You have everything that you need to solve every problem that you have, but it's within you, buried under layers of the past, bitterness and resentment. Work with someone who will assist you with becoming a better version of yourself.

Sometimes you have to make room for Bigger things in your life. Dream Big then Dream Bigger.

Have you stopped dreaming because of what happened to you in the past or the hard work that it takes to bring a dream to reality? Keshelle Davis, Master Dreamer and Law of Attraction enthusiast, feels that people don't take the steps to make their dreams a reality, because (1) they are too busy working on their job; (2) they are too afraid to step out of their comfort zone and do something different; and (3) because the long process to make a dream come true frustrates people. It's more comfortable to stay in misery than to keep striving for excellence.

Keshelle recommends that you give yourself permission to dream. Write the vision and make it plain. Get clear to the point that you can physically see what your vision will look like. Once you have the vision, create a vision board/dream board by cutting out pictures of what you desire and putting them where you can see them regularly. This should keep you energized and moving forward towards making your dream a reality.

There is Always Room at the Top. To demonstrate I drove to the top of the parking garage as the bottom is always crowded. I was not surprised. The long lines of competition is for mediocrity. Very few compete for the top. As a matter of fact, we were alone. Be a minority on the ladder of success. Just go to the top!!!

Is it easier to fight others for lower level positions or fight to go to the top? Either way, there will be competition. You might as well use your energy to go towards excellence.

My advice is stop worrying about making the right decision. Make a decision and then make it become the right decision.

Making a decision is hard for some people and they'd rather have a root canal than make the wrong decision. The fear of making a decision can be paralyzing, but the effects of indecision are just as worse. Instead of procrastinating for fear of making the wrong decision, make a decision and then work hard to make it right. At least you'll be moving towards your intended goal.

Most would think that shopping and buying what you want, when you want brings joy and is a display of freedom. Because I have experienced both sides of this coin I can tell you that it's not true. For me, the happiness is when I don't have the things, but achieving the goal that allows me to get the things. That's where the real happiness is. It's in the process of achieving.

All the money in the world won't make you happy, although you may want to test that theory for yourself. The insight from Mr. Buggs comes from someone who has a great net worth, so his advice is valid. Happiness is going after the goal and Becoming who you need to be to reach it. As you get close to achieving your big goals, it's time to set new and bigger goals.

I read an article about someone who recently became a billionaire after selling a well-known video game. He was sad and pseudo-depressed about the life the money created. He didn't know who his real friends were and his girlfriend left him, saying she wanted someone "normal." I wonder if he didn't have another goal set up or a way to use his money to serve the greater good.

A great example of aiming higher is Elon Musk. When he makes money, he reinvests it in bigger and more innovative projects. There are no limits to happiness, but shift your focus from the money and put it in the process of achieving what others told you was impossible.

It's free to dream, but very expensive when you don't.

Dreaming is free, yet many people have limited themselves and stopped dreaming. In school, we were scolded for day dreaming, but everything that is in existence today started with a dream. The chair you sit in was a dream in someone's mind. Amazon and Kindle were dreams.

Are you limiting yourself and your possibilities in life by not dreaming? Dreaming is F-R-E-E and will only cost you time and effort. Why not start today and uncover the dreams buried in your mind and heart that are waiting for you to bring them to the world.

Keeping your vision in front of you is critical. My philosophy has been that if I am sitting or standing, I am reading my goals, if I am driving or sleeping, I am listening to my goals!!! I only have 24 hours in a day. I just used more of those hours than most to train my mind on where to take me. I'm not better than most, just more disciplined!

What goals have you set for yourself? What do you want your life to look like in two years personally and professionally? Do you want to be healthier? Want less stress? A closer connection with your family? Less drama with your spouse or children?

Mr. Buggs is giving you the actions to retrain and reprogram your mind for high levels of success. Your mindset is greatly affected by what you read, listen to and watch. What are you doing with your 24 hours each day?

Chapter 9

Les Brown

During some of my challenging times as an entrepreneur, I watched Les Brown's videos on YouTube over and over and over again. I got his audiobook, *The Power of Purpose*, and have listened to it countless times. Les Brown is entertaining and insightful and will give you the courage to shift out of your comfort zone and into your greatness. He's had profound impact on my life and ability to stay in the journey of entrepreneurship. He can do the same for you!

*Leslie (Les) Brown and his twin brother were born on the floor in an abandoned building in Liberty City, Miami in 1945. Their natural mother became pregnant while her husband was away at war and couldn't keep the babies. They were adopted by Miss Mamie Brown, who although only had a 3rd-grade education, she had the heart to love and raise children.

Les was mistakenly declared, "educable mentally retarded," in elementary school and carried that label all throughout high school. Mistaken for his brother one day in class, a teacher told him to go to the chalkboard and work a math problem. After hesitating several times, he finally told the teacher that he was the "dumb twin" and couldn't work the problem because he was educable mentally retarded. The teacher told him, "Don't you ever let someone's opinion of you become your reality." That day changed his life.

He used determination, persistence, and belief to go beyond being a sanitation worker, to unleash a lifetime of amazing achievements, including becoming a broadcast station manager, political commentator, multi-term state representative in Ohio and international motivational speaker.

Les Brown is one of the world's most renowned motivational speakers and is highly sought after by Fortune 500 companies, small business owners, non-profits and other community leaders. He's spoken to audiences as large as 80,000 and inspires people to stop being complacent, aim high and actively make an impact on the world. He's been awarded some of the highest honors from top speaking organizations, including being voted as "One of the Top Five Outstanding Speakers," by Toastmasters International and the "Golden Gavel Award" for achievement and leadership in communication by the National Speakers Association.

He's authored several *New York Times* bestselling books and his YouTube videos are watched by hundreds of thousands of people around the world. (source LesBrown.com)
******

You are never too old to set another goal or to dream a new dream.

If you're paying attention, there are 10 – 15-year-olds building multi-million dollar companies. Whether they're selling lemonade, bowties, bottled water or sneakers, there are lots of stories of young entrepreneurs. They pursued their dreams without fear of failure and ridicule of others. I'm sure they had challenges, but as adults, the fear of looking bad during failure stops plenty of people from stepping out on their dreams.

NOW is always a great time to start on your dream. You're never too old or too young. It just takes action, perseverance and a plan.

Chaleo Yoovidhya created Red Bull at 61. Julia Child wrote her first cookbook when she was 50. Martha Stewart started catering in her mid-30's and was nearly 50 before signing a deal to create the Martha Stewart Living magazine.

If you fall, make sure you fall on your back, because if you can look up, you can get up.

Failure is a part of life. You won't die if you fail, but will be better because of it, since you learned something new about yourself and/or other people. Make sure you're able to look up and give thanks when you fall down. There is ALWAYS a lesson in failure.

When you are negative, you're sending out negative energy and you're blocking your good.
Some people walk around with a natural growl on their face. They are angry before and after they've had their coffee and often wonder why they're lonely. They use loneliness as a reason to continue to be negative. Is this you?

When you're negative, you repel people and you also repel good things. You stop good things from happening because of the negative energy emanating from your body. Become more conscious of your energy and free yourself from negativity.

Work your dream until it gets hot. See, most things don't happen as soon as we think they should happen. The Messenger of Misery might drop in on you and say "Hello." Murphy's Law might come by and thump you on the head. Any number of things can happen to interrupt your flow, it's okay. Don't take it personal.
Most people think that wealthy people became successful overnight. There are plenty of get rich quick schemes out there, and ads on social media promising six-figures in six months if you follow their simple plan. Do you quit and give up if you aren't successful in 30 days? Do you give minimal effort to your goals and then get frustrated because you failed?

Achieving success is hard enough when you're giving full effort. Go after everything that you desire in life and expect bumps along the way. Take them graciously, learn, get back up and continue. Understand that it's just a part of the process and happens to ALL great people.

Some people have to hit rock bottom in order to rise.
Sometimes it takes you to have nothing else behind you in order to take action to change your life. When you have nothing left to lose, and you didn't die because you lost it all, it can serve

as the greatest catalyst to change. Don't despise the crisis, study it. It may have come to shift you out of your comfortable state and make you into who you were meant to be to serve the world.

Make no apologies for pursuing your greatest life. Take ownership of your life and make a conscious choice to align your words, feelings, and actions to make your dream a reality. Life is calling you up higher. Continue to stretch yourself and rise to the occasion.

To rise higher and be happier, you must get your words, feelings, and actions into alignment. Do you say that you don't care about being in a relationship, but you're secretly lonely and look to meet someone at a restaurant or networking event? Your words are out of alignment with your actions and feelings.

Do you say you're happy, but drink regularly to numb the pain of your misery? Your actions and feelings aren't in alignment with what you're saying. To create real change, Speak how you want to Feel and then take Action to make it a reality. Get into alignment and watch how fast your life will change for the best.

Sometimes when you have outgrown the situations in your life, and you are not aware or do not have the courage to move on, life will move on you. You may have been told that your company is going in another direction. You knew it was coming, and you didn't prepare yourself. Now you are angry and feel you were wronged.

Don't I know this to be true! It was time for me to move from my career because I felt like I was being minimized and wasn't happy. It took time to realize that life moved on me and created that situation for my exit. After that, I forgave everyone for how the "story" played out.

If you have energy stirring around in you and it's trying to get out, sometimes your outer circumstances will change and facilitate the movement of that energy. The challenge is realizing what looks like a crisis, is actually an opportunity for you to live the life you desire.

Start making preparation, downsize your lifestyle and start seeking other opportunities before life moves on you...because eventually it will.

When you are willing to throw it all on the line, that's when life takes on a whole new dimension. Most people won't do that.

The more you want in life and the greater you desire to become, failure will be a natural part of the process. If you realize that most highly successful people failed (epically) before achieving success, then you won't feel like a loser when it happens to you. Failure is a stepping stone on the way to achievement. Find the lesson in your failure and apply it in your next attempt. If you quit after the first try, do you really deserve success?

Be bold! In order to receive much, you must risk much. Don't worry about what your critics say. Most of them wish they were you anyway. Think "bigger." Be unreasonable! Abandon logic. Forget about being rational! If your dream is unrealistic, go for it! We all know today anything is possible.

Are you the smartest person in your circle at work? Are you biggest fish in your pond of friends. Do you want more and feel like you can be better than you are?

How can you achieve your goals if you are stuck around people who are just like you? Everyone knows just as much as the next person. Either you are all the same size, or you are bigger in certain areas.

Have you ever seen the image of the fish jumping out of a bowl full of fish into a new and larger bowl alone? That's similar to what it's like in life. Are you willing to jump into a new bowl that's larger than where you are now? There are people who are squirming by playing small for the world and there are others who have become comfortable with being uncomfortable.

The problem is when you blame other people or complain about something that you can change. It's time to jump!! Jump into a new pond with new possibilities. Go NOW!

Stress can shut down your power if you let it. Don't allow people, bills, or pressures on the job to consume your focus, energy, and joy for life. Uncontrolled stress can cause you to gain weight, change your personality, create problems in your relationships, turn your hair gray overnight, make you sick, and make it difficult for you to get out of bed.

Unmanaged stress and anxiety can ruin your life. In addition to digging an early grave, your relationships are greatly affected. According to the National Institute of Health (NIH), "Emotional stress is a major contributing factor to the six leading causes of death in the U.S.: cancer, coronary heart disease, accidental injuries, respiratory disorders, cirrhosis of the liver and suicide." Prolonged and unmanaged stress causes many health ailments including autoimmune disorders, which include multiple sclerosis, arthritis, lupus and Type 1 diabetes.

Do you have strained relationships, because you are unable to manage your emotions around others? Do you avoid your family during the holidays, because you don't want to be a part of their drama? You may be missing out on the best times with your family because of your anxiety. Seek a coach or assistance to uncover and resolve the root cause of your anxiety. The solutions to your issues cannot be found in a bottle of wine, alcohol or medication. Don't just self-medicate the symptoms. Solve the root and change your life for the best.

Chapter 10

Maya Angelou

It's hard to quantify the impact that Dr. Maya Angelou has had on my life. Growing up as a young black girl from the south, I saw her as an example of a positive and influential black woman, who had become highly successful. Signaling to me that it was possible too.

As my life and career started to unravel a few years ago, I bought Oprah's 25th Anniversary DVD set. Oprah had a slumber party with her and they talked while they laid in bed. Maya Angelou said, "On the other side of every storm is a greater sense of joy." I felt like my life was a living hell, but her words provided me comfort and I believed her. Joy on the other side of the storm. That meant the storm couldn't last forever and I had something to look forward to. What would the greater joy be? I recorded her saying that on my phone, and listened to it again and again when I was having difficult times at work, sometimes over 20 times a day.

My life today is the joy that was on the other side of the storm. Who could have imagined that it would be this INCREDIBLE! You never know how one statement can make such an impact in someone's life. Powerful!

*American poet, memoirist, and civil rights activist, Marguerite Ann Johnson, was born in 1928, in St. Louis, Missouri. When she was seven years old, she was raped by her mother's boyfriend. Shortly after telling her brother who did it, the police found him dead; apparently kicked to death by her male relatives. Devastated that "her voice" killed him, she stopped talking and was eventually sent back to Arkansas to live with her paternal grandmother. The people in the area called her dumb, a moron, idiot and stupid.

Her grandmother always spoke highly of her, to her and others. Her grandmother's friend, a teacher, took Dr. Angelou under her wing. She introduced her to a little library and asked her to read a large number of books and write reports on what she'd read. Through this, she discovered poetry and fell in love with it. The teacher eventually coaxed her into talking, six years after she stopped, by telling her that poetry had to be felt through speaking.

Before graduating from high school, she worked as the first black female streetcar conductor in San Francisco. When she began her career as a nightclub singer, she took the professional name, Maya Angelou, combining her childhood nickname with a form of her husband's name. She was active in the Civil Rights movement and befriended Martin Luther King Jr. and Malcolm X. After Dr. King was assassinated, she fell into a deep depression. She also felt great pain after Malcolm X was assassinated.

Dr. Angelou channeled the pain of her life's experiences into her 1969 memoir, *I Know Why The Caged Bird Sings*, which made literary history as the first non-fiction best-seller by an African-American woman. Over the span of 50 years, Dr. Angelou wrote 30 books, spoke 6 languages, won 3 Grammy's, and was the 2nd poet in history to recite a poem at a Presidential Inauguration. She received dozens of awards and more than 50 honorary degrees from colleges and universities.

In 2010, President Barack Obama awarded Dr. Maya Angelou the nation's highest civilian honor, the Presidential Medal of Freedom. She died on May 28, 2014. (source Biography.com)
******

Bitterness is like cancer. It eats upon the host, it does nothing to the object of its displeasure.

Did someone do something to you in the past and you feel that you can't move forward in certain areas of your life because of it? Is that true? Is that person physically stopping you from moving forward or is it the story?

Holding on to the past and not forgiving people will eat away at your soul. Holding on to guilt, shame, resentment, and bitterness don't affect the other person's life. They've likely moved on, but you still hold the weight of what happened. Free yourself and move forward into a new and exciting future.

The thing to do, it seems to me, is to prepare yourself so that you can become a rainbow in somebody else's cloud.

In order to be a rainbow in somebody else's cloud, you have to work to BECOME a better person. That means resolving your past, embracing your fears, ignoring the naysayers and stepping into your destiny.

What challenges have you overcome in your life that you can assist others with today? Being a single parent, or a father fighting for visitation/custody? Rising from poverty and uneducated communities? You have the ability to impact a number of people where you are today and an infinite number of people when you do the work to Become who you were meant to be. How are you using it to better the lives of others?

Some day they will be able to measure the power of words. I think they are things. I think they get on the walls. They get in your wallpaper. They get in your rugs and your upholstery and your clothes and finally into you.

Words are so powerful, yet many people are not mindful about what they say about themselves or others. When you call a child names, your words can vibrate in their soul, and show up in a dysfunction 30 years later. How are you speaking to your family, spouse or co-workers? How do you treat the cashier or the person who makes your lunch when you're in a hurry?

Become conscious of your language and make an effort to speak life into yourself and others.

I am a teacher. I teach all the time, as you do, and as all of us do. Whether we know it or not, whether we take responsibility for it or not. I hold nothing back.

As a leader, people are watching you all the time. Whether or not you acknowledge you're a leader, you are to someone. Whether it's your children, spouse, family members or colleagues, people are watching. People at the coffee shop watch how you interact with the staff. People are also watching how you treat others on the train or the bus.

What are you teaching others with your actions? What are you sharing with them that can improve their lives with your words? Take responsibility for being a teacher and leader in the lives of others and do your part in making the world a better place.

Maybe that's the hardest part. If you teach, you have to live your teaching. You can't say, "You do not as I do, but do as I say." No. No. You have to say, "I'm doing my best to live what I teach."

Do you live the advice that you are giving out to others? Are you taking advice from people who don't live theirs? There are plenty of ads on social media of people who say they will teach you how to become rich, but are they broke and getting rich by teaching something they haven't demonstrated in their own lives? I saw a health coach, near my southern hometown, who was seriously overweight. I'm not judging her for being overweight, but what advice is she sharing with others that she's not taking?

As you offer guidance and insight to others, ensure that you're actually living what you're teaching. As you take advice, make sure people have the results you desire.

You know what's right. Just do right. You really don't have to ask anybody. The truth is right. May not be expedient, it may not be profitable, but it will satisfy your soul.

For the most part, we have been taught the difference between right and wrong. You can also sense what's right for you as you make decisions based on how you feel about yourself. When you make a decision and get a sick feeling in your stomach, it's not the right decision. Sometimes the truth takes longer and doesn't make everyone happy, but your soul will be at rest.

When someone shows you who they are the first time, believe them.
Character shows up in a person's actions towards you and others. This is especially true when it comes to dating and friendships. We tend to overlook the faults in others and are shocked when that fault is multiplied and more egregious later.

I remember going on a first date with this guy and he told me to decide where we were going to eat that day because I wasn't going to be able to decide later in our relationship. *Wait a minute..... Won't be able to decide later? Relationship?* We had just met a few days before that and he was telling me that he was a controlling lunatic. Did I hear it? Did I believe him? YES I DID and that was the only meal we shared.

How many times have you given someone the benefit of the doubt and somehow found yourself in a predicament later? Become more alert at judging a person's character when they show you who they are the first time.

I never had that feeling that I had to carry the weight of somebody's ignorance around with me. And that was true for racists who wanted to use the 'n' word when talking about me or about my people, or the stupidity of people who really wanted to belittle other folks, because they weren't pretty or they weren't rich or they weren't clever.
There is a lot of negativity in the world and on social media. There are a lot of people freely expressing their hate and ignorance towards others. Are you letting them affect you and then carrying the anger, offense and hate around with you? Are you carrying the unnecessary baggage of the ignorance and shortcomings of others?

How does this impact them? It doesn't. However, your life and the lives of those around you are greatly impacted. Ignore people, forgive them and don't engage in meaningless debates with people you don't know.

If a human being dreams a great dream. Dares to love somebody. If a human being dares to be Martin King or Mahatma Gandhi or Mother Teresa or Malcolm X. If a human being dares to be bigger than the condition into which she or he was born, it means so can you.

If you dare to be bigger than who you are today and UNLEASH your greatness, the world will never be the same. If your soul is stirring around, silently shouting, "Let me out," answer the call and Become the world leader you were meant to be.

Pick up the battle and make it a better world. Just where you are. Yes, and it can be better. It must be better, but it is up to us.

You have everything that you need to fulfill the dream that's stirring in your heart. You are adequately prepared at this moment to take the first step, but you must take ACTION. You don't need more time, more money or some magic wand to make it happen. All you need to do is to DECIDE that it is time for you to Become who you were meant to be and take the first step.

After that, doors will start to open and opportunities will come across your path that you could have never imagined. The world is waiting for you. Will you pick up the battle? Even if you start locally. Your community is waiting for you.

How will you be remembered when you're on your death bed? Did you live? Did you give? Did you matter? It's not too late. Start where you are. Go NOW in the direction of your dreams!

Closing

I hope that this book was useful to you and was valuable for the time you invested in reading it. I have learned so much from these leaders and wanted to share their insight and knowledge with more people around the world.

Most of them have books, videos, audios and a host of other resources that will assist you with the challenges that life brings. I'm so happy that you've joined me on this journey of unfolding and discovery. I'm excited about what your future holds.

Keep me informed of your progress! Send me an e-mail and connect with me on social media.

My links are:
Web: www.christyrutherford.com
Private Community – www.restoreuwithChristy.com
Email: liveupleadership@gmail.com

To your success, happiness and unlimited joy!!

About The Author

Christy Rutherford is a Leadership and Success Coach and President of LIVE-UP Leadership, a leadership development and training company. Christy is also a certified Executive Leadership Coach and assists companies with creating cultures of high performance.

Christy Rutherford served over 16 years as an active duty Coast Guard officer and is the 13th African American woman to achieve the rank of O-5 in the Coast Guard's 245+ year history. Her tours expanded from: drug interdictions on the high seas; emergency response/dispatch to hundreds of major/minor maritime accidents; enforcing federal laws on 100's of oil/hazardous material companies; responding to the needs of the citizens in New Orleans two days after Hurricane Katrina; a Congressional Fellowship with the House of Representatives and lastly a position that benefited from her wide range of experience.

A Harvard Business School Alumna from the Program for Leadership Development, Christy also earned a Bachelor of Science in Agricultural Business from South Carolina State University, a Master of Business Administration from Averett University, a Diploma Sous Chef de Patisserie from Alain and Marie Lenotre Culinary Institute, and a Certification in Executive Leadership Coaching from Georgetown University.

Among her many professional accomplishments, her national recognition includes the Coast Guard Dorothy Stratton Leadership Award, Cambridge Who's Who Amongst Executives and Professionals, Career Communications STEM Technology All-Star and the Edward R. Williams Award for Excellence In Diversity.

A speaker and best-selling author, Christy recently released four books, *Shackled To Success, Heal Your Brokenness, Philosophies of Iconic Leaders* and *Philosophies of Spiritual Leaders*.

Made in the USA
Columbia, SC
23 July 2022